THE DARK KNIGHT

Screenplay by
Jonathan Nolan and Christopher Nolan

Story by Christopher Nolan & David S. Goyer

Batman created by Bob Kane

LEVEL 3

SCHOLASTIC

Adapted by: Jane Revell

Publisher: Jacquie Bloese

Editor: Fiona Beddall

Designer: Dawn Wilson

Cover layout: Eddie Rego

Photo credits:
Cover and interior images provided courtesy of Warner Bros. Entertainment, Inc.

Published by Scholastic Ltd. 2009

Mary Glasgow Magazines (Scholastic Ltd.)
Euston House
24 Eversholt Street
London NW1 IDB

Printed in Singapore. Reprinted in 2010.

CONTENTS

ON THE SIDE OF THE LAW

BRUCE WAYNE is the rich owner

of Wayne Enterprises. He seems to be interested only in beautiful women and fast cars. In secret, he is the Batman, who fights crime and protects people. He has been in love with Rachel Dawes for a long time.

ALFRED PENNYWORTH is Bruce's

assistant. He has worked for the Wayne family for years, and has known Bruce since he was a boy.

LUCIUS FOX is the director of

Wayne Enterprises. He is great with technology. He designed the Batmobile and the Batsuit.

LIEUTENANT JAMES GORDON

is one of the top police officers in Gotham City. He has used Batman's help in the past. He has a wife, Barbara, and two small children.

DETECTIVE RAMIREZ AND DETECTIVE WUERTZ are police officers who work for Lieutenant Gordon in the Gotham City Police Station.

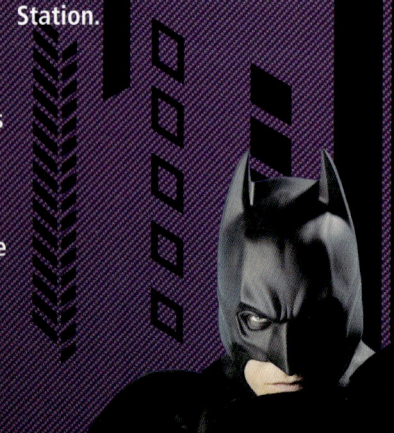

HARVEY DENT is the new District Attorney*. He is in love with Rachel Dawes. He wants to stop criminals and make Gotham City a safe place to live.

RACHEL DAWES is an Assistant District Attorney. Harvey Dent is her boss – and her boyfriend. She's known Bruce since they were children, and she knows he is Batman.

THE CRIMINALS

◀ **THE JOKER** is crazy and dangerous. For him, hurting people is a game and killing people is fun. He hides his face with white make-up and a horrible big red smile. What is he hiding? What does he want?

SAL MARONI is the boss of the Mob** in Gotham. He's the man behind a lot of the crime in the city. His men are thieves and murderers.

MR LAU is the director of the Hong Kong company LSI Holdings, but is he an honest man?

PLACES

GOTHAM CITY is a large, modern city with big problems. There is a lot of crime, and people can't always trust their politicians and the police.

BRUCE'S FLAT is at the top of a very high building. He moved there after one of his enemies burned down his huge family house.

THE BAT-BUNKER is Batman's secret room deep under the ground. He keeps his Batmobile there, and a lot of computers and equipment too.

* District Attorney: a very important lawyer who works for the US government; in many parts of the USA, people vote to choose their District Attorney

** the Mob: another word for the Mafia – a group of dangerous criminals who work together closely

PROLOGUE

Police Lieutenant* James Gordon stood on top of the tall police station in Gotham City. He was looking up at a huge shape of a bat against the night sky. There was light all around it. Gordon smiled. The Bat-Signal. It meant that Batman was looking after Gotham City and protecting its people.

A young policewoman named Anna Ramirez came out. She gave Gordon a cup of coffee.

Ramirez looked at the Bat-Signal. 'I hear that you're going to catch Batman soon.'

* Lieutenant: a high position in the police

Gordon gave a half smile. Some people in Gotham were afraid of Batman because he often broke the law. The police had instructions to catch him, but Gordon didn't want to. Batman helped him in the fight against crime and kept the city safe. Gordon used the Bat-Signal to call him. They had a sort of friendship. The other police officers knew this, so they didn't try too hard to discover who Batman was.

'Didn't he come tonight?' asked Detective Ramirez.

'He's probably busy,' said Gordon. 'But it's good for people to remember that he's out there somewhere.'

CHAPTER 1
Robbers at the bank

On the street in front of Gotham First National Bank, three bank robbers were getting ready. In a big room at the back of the bank, millions of dollars were waiting for them. All three men were wearing clown masks with white faces and big red mouths. All three carried guns and little bombs.

'Is it just the three of us?' asked the robber called Chuckles.

'No, there are two more on the roof,' said the one called Grumpy.

'That means five people to share the money,' said Chuckles.

'No, six,' said Bozo. 'There's the Joker too – the guy who planned the job.'

Up on the roof, the robber named Dopey had just switched off the security system.

'I'm finished here,' he said.

'Yes, you are,' said Happy. He took out his gun and shot Dopey. Then he grabbed the bags and ran down into the bank.

The three robbers in the street ran into the bank shooting. Chuckles hit the security guard on the head with his gun. The guard fell to the floor. Grumpy and Bozo pushed all the people in the bank together. They gave everyone a little bomb and took out all the pins.

'Keep very still,' they said. 'Those bombs will explode if you move.'

At the back of the bank, Happy was opening the large metal door to the room with all the money. Grumpy came to join him.

'What kind of a bank is this?' asked Happy.

'A Mob bank,' said Grumpy. 'What happened to Dopey?'

'The Joker told me to kill him,' said Happy.

'That's funny,' said Grumpy. 'The Joker told me to kill *you*.' He took out his gun and shot Happy. Then he started putting money into the bags.

When Grumpy went to the front of the bank again, he saw Chuckles' body. Only he and Bozo were left.

'You're going to kill me, aren't you?' he said to Bozo.

'No,' said Bozo. 'I'm going to kill the bus driver.'

'Bus driver? What bus …?'

Suddenly a yellow school bus crashed through the window. It threw Grumpy across the room and killed him immediately. Bozo shot the driver. Now he was alone. He put all the money into the bus and climbed into the driver's seat. Then he turned to look at the people. They were still holding the bombs and they were shaking.

The clown began to laugh, quietly at first, then louder and louder. Suddenly he tore off his clown mask. It was Gotham's newest and most feared criminal – the Joker.

Lieutenant Gordon stood in the middle of Gotham First National Bank. There was a huge hole in the wall, and all around him was broken glass. The police had rescued everybody and turned off the bombs. They had found five bodies, all wearing clown masks. Now Gordon's officers were asking people questions.

Detective Ramirez showed Gordon some photos. 'They were taken by the bank's security cameras,' she said.

Gordon looked at the photos. The Joker looked like a clown, even without his clown mask. His skin was covered in white make-up, his hair was green, and a big red smile was painted across his face. He didn't look funny. He looked scary.

Gordon heard a noise behind him. He turned around. It was Batman.

'Give us a moment, please,' he shouted to his officers. They moved away.

Gordon showed Batman the photos. Batman knew the Joker's face from other crimes in the city.

'Him again,' he said. 'Who are the others?'

'Just ordinary criminals. Nobodies,' said Gordon.

Batman picked up some money from the floor.

'These are some of the marked notes that I gave you,' he said. Batman had marked the notes in a special way, to find out which banks the Mob was using.

'We used the notes last week to buy guns from the Mob,' said Gordon. 'We've found four other banks where the Mob does business.'

'Then it's time to take their money,' said Batman. He knew that they had to stop the Mob. Gotham could only be safe if the Mob was finished.

'We'll have to attack all the banks at the same time. And we'll have to talk to the new District Attorney first.'

'Is he a good man?' asked Batman.

'He's got very strong ideas,' said Gordon, looking again at the notes. 'Like you.'

Gordon looked up, but Batman had gone.

Bruce Wayne was in his secret room deep under the ground – the Bat-Bunker. In the middle of the room was the Batmobile. Behind it, the wall was completely covered with television screens and computers.

Bruce was watching the screens when he heard the noisy lift coming down. He wasn't worried. Only one other man knew about this place. Alfred had looked after the Wayne family for years, and was Bruce's assistant and friend.

As he put a pot of coffee in front of Bruce, Alfred looked at one of the screens.

'That's Harvey Dent, the new District Attorney, isn't it?' he said.

'Yes,' replied Bruce. 'I wonder if we can trust him.'

He looked at different pictures of Harvey Dent on the screens. In one video, Dent was helping a woman out of a taxi. The woman was Bruce's friend, Rachel Dawes. The couple disappeared into a restaurant.

'Are you interested in Dent's politics, or his women friends?' asked Alfred.

'Rachel's the Assistant District Attorney. It's no surprise that she and Dent spend time together,' said Bruce unhappily.

Alfred poured Bruce a cup of coffee. 'Be careful, sir,' he said. 'Don't try to do too much.'

'Batman can do anything,' said Bruce.

'That's not true, sir,' said Alfred, and he turned back towards the lift.

Gordon walked into the District Attorney's office.

'I want to meet Batman,' said Harvey Dent from behind his desk. 'I know you're working with him.'

'Batman is a law breaker, wanted by the police,' said Gordon, repeating the words that Dent always used with reporters. 'I'll tell you when we've found him.' Then he changed the subject. 'I want to search five banks, and I need the right papers from your office.'

'Who are you chasing?' asked Dent.

'I can't tell you that yet,' Gordon replied.

'The information's safe with *me*, Gordon. It's your cops* who are working for the Mob.'

Gordon didn't answer. He knew that Dent might be right. In his last job, Dent had found out a lot of bad things about Gotham's police officers.

'I can give you the names of the banks,' Gordon said finally.

'Well, that's a start,' said Dent. 'I'll get you the papers … but I want your trust.'

'I trust you,' said Gordon. 'We all know that you're Gotham's White Knight.'

'I hear the police have a different name for me.'

'Yes,' thought Gordon. 'And not a very nice one.' But he just smiled at Dent.

* cop: another word for police officer

CHAPTER 2
The Mob gets angry

Lucius Fox, director of Wayne Enterprises, took Mr Lau to the lift after their meeting. Mr Lau was the director of the Hong Kong company LSI Holdings, and he wanted their two companies to do business together. The meeting had been interesting, but with one problem: the third person there, Bruce Wayne, had been asleep.

When Fox got back to the meeting room, Bruce was awake. He was standing by a large window.

'Another long night?' Fox asked. He knew what Bruce did at night. Fox had worked for many years in the design department at Wayne Enterprises, and had designed the Batsuit and the Batmobile for him.

Bruce smiled.

'I'm not sure that we should work with Mr Lau,' said Fox. 'He's making too much money. I think he's a criminal.'

'I agree,' said Bruce. 'I wasn't really interested in doing business with him. I just wanted to see his bank records.'

As Fox turned to go, Bruce said, 'I need a new suit.'

Fox looked at him. 'Yes, that suit's not really in fashion.'

'I don't mean *this* suit, Lucius,' said Bruce. 'I'm talking about my *Bat*suit.' He showed Fox some designs. 'I need to be able to turn my head more easily,' he explained.

Fox took the designs. 'I'll see what I can do,' he said.

Bruce walked into Gotham's most popular new restaurant. He knew that Rachel was there tonight with Harvey Dent. He wanted to see her … and he wanted to see Dent.

'Do you think this suit is out of fashion, Natasha?' he

asked the beautiful Russian dancer at his side. She just smiled.

Bruce saw Rachel and Dent and walked towards their table. 'Rachel!' he said. 'What a surprise!'

Rachel had known Bruce Wayne all her life. She knew this wasn't a surprise for him.

The women kissed and the men shook hands.

'Why don't we have dinner together?' suggested Bruce.

'It's never easy to get a table here,' said Dent quickly. He didn't want to share Rachel with anyone that night. 'I don't think the waiters will …'

Bruce didn't let him finish. He owned the restaurant. The waiters always did what he asked.

While Rachel and Natasha talked about dancing, Harvey and Bruce talked about Gotham City. Dent really wanted to stop the criminals. He wanted to make Gotham a safe place to live.

'I don't think Batman wants to look after us for ever,' Dent said. 'I think he would like someone else to take his place.'

Bruce agreed. Perhaps Harvey Dent was that man, but only if he continued as District Attorney. If Dent wanted to get Gotham's vote a second time, he would need money.

'Why don't we have a little party?' he said. 'We can ask all my friends to write you a cheque.'

It was an invitation that Harvey Dent could not refuse.

While Bruce Wayne and Harvey Dent were having dinner together, leaders of the Mob were meeting in a hotel in the city centre. Sal Maroni, the Mob boss, was sitting at a table with two other criminals, the Chechen and Gambol. Each man had his own guards. On a screen in the middle of the table, Mr Lau was speaking.

'As you know,' Lau was saying, 'the Joker stole our money from Gotham First National Bank. Luckily it wasn't much. Only sixty-eight million dollars.'

'The Joker's not the problem,' said Maroni. 'He's a nobody. The problem is that the notes were marked. My spies in the police say that they are going to attack our other banks today.'

'We need to move the money,' said Lau. 'Let's move it to my company in Hong Kong.'

The three men around the table didn't like that idea. They didn't trust Lau.

Suddenly there was a mad laugh from the back of the room. The laugh got louder and louder and the Joker appeared.

'Your money won't be safe in Hong Kong. Batman will find Lau and make him talk,' the Joker said. 'I've got a much better idea. Kill Batman. I'll do it for you … for a price.'

'How much do you want?' the Chechen asked angrily.

'Half.'

The criminals were amazed. They couldn't believe that the Joker wanted half of their money.

'Why don't I just kill *you*?' said Gambol.

'If you did, you would all die too,' said the Joker. He opened his jacket. There was a bomb on his chest.

'Think about it,' he said, and he walked out of the room.

Now the criminals needed to protect their money from the Joker too. Maroni turned to Lau.

'How soon can you move the money?' he asked.

'I've already moved it,' said Lau. The camera pulled back to show Lau sitting on a plane. He was on his way to Hong Kong with all the Mob's money.

The mob leaders shouted at him angrily, but it was too late.

Across town, Lieutenant Gordon was angry too. His police officers had gone into five different Gotham City banks, but the money was gone.

The Bat-Signal shone brightly in the evening sky. This time, Batman came. He landed on the roof of the police station. But it wasn't Lieutenant Gordon waiting for him. It was Harvey Dent.

Suddenly the roof door flew open and Gordon arrived. He was angry that someone else was using the Bat-Signal.

'Lau's on his way to Hong Kong,' Dent said to Gordon. 'Why didn't you tell me about him earlier? I can take away people's passports if I know that they might be criminals.'

'They knew we were coming,' said Gordon. 'There must be a spy in your office.'

'*My* office?' said Dent. 'It's *your* detectives who are working for the Mob!'

Batman moved closer. This was not a good time for differences.

'Lau must come back,' Dent said to Batman, 'but the Chinese won't give him to us. Bring him to me, and I'll make him talk.'

'If you go against the Mob, they will try to kill you,' Gordon told Dent.

'I know the dangers,' said Dent.

'How will you get Lau back?' Dent asked Batman.

But Batman had gone.

Lucius Fox showed Batman his new Batsuit.

'It's lighter and faster than the old one,' he said, 'and it can move more easily. But there's a problem with that. It means that there are weak parts. It will be easier for a knife or gun to kill you.'

'Well, we don't want to make things too easy, do we?' said Bruce.

He was very happy with the new suit. There were even knives on the arms! He pressed a little black button.

WHOOSH! Three disks flew out from the arm and shot across the room. They nearly cut off Bruce's ear. Fox laughed at the surprise on Bruce's face.

'Um … it's always a good idea to read the instructions first,' he said.

Bruce went very red. 'Sorry,' he said.

Fox put the suit back in the cupboard and locked it again.

'Would you like to go to Hong Kong to talk to Mr Lau?' asked Bruce.

'What's wrong with a phone call?' said Fox.

CHAPTER 3
Lau's surprise journey

Lucius Fox arrived at LSI Holdings in Hong Kong.

'I'm afraid I have to ask you for your mobile phone,' said a security guard. He took it and put it in a box under the desk.

Fox was taken into his breakfast meeting with Mr Lau.

'Good morning, Mr Fox,' said Lau as he poured his guest an orange juice. 'I'm so sorry I had to leave Gotham in a hurry. But we can continue here.'

'Yes,' said Fox. 'I've come to …'

Brrrinnng. Brrrinnng. A mobile phone rang. Fox put his hand in his pocket and pulled out a second mobile phone.

'Sorry,' he said as he switched it off.

'We do not allow mobile phones in here,' said Lau.

'I'd forgotten that I had it,' said Fox. 'Mr Lau, we've decided not to work with you. I'm here to tell you why.'

Fox explained things to Lau and stood up. Lau was very angry. Fox picked up his mobile phone and walked out. At the security desk, the guard offered him back his phone. Fox shook his head and showed the guard the phone in his hand. The guard looked surprised, then put Fox's phone back in the box under the desk.

Bruce was waiting for Fox on a narrow bridge in the centre of Hong Kong.

'Is it easy to get into LSI Holdings?' he asked.

'No, but this will help,' said Fox. He showed Bruce the phone that he had taken into his meeting with Lau. When he touched the screen, it showed a 3D map of Lau's office. Bruce was amazed.

'I left another phone there this morning,' said Fox. 'It's sending out pictures.'

'Thank you, Lucius,' said Bruce, as he began to walk away.

'Good luck, Mr Wayne,' said Fox.

It was dark. Batman was waiting on the roof of the building opposite LSI Holdings. His new Batsuit felt very comfortable. It moved easily, like a second skin. He could turn his head better too.

Batman shot a gun four times at Lau's office window. A small bomb came out each time and stuck to the glass. Their clocks started: 2:24, 2:23, 2:22 …

Inside LSI Holdings, in the box under the security desk, a blue light switched on on Fox's phone. All the lights in the building went out and the security doors unlocked and opened. The phone in Lau's hand went dead and he was suddenly very afraid. He grabbed a gun from his desk and ran into the hall screaming in Chinese, 'Where are the police? What am I paying them for?'

Batman jumped into the air. The Batsuit's wings opened and he flew across to Lau's building. He went in through a large window and made his way to Lau's office. The door was locked so he kicked it in. Lau shot at him, but Batman was on top of him in a second. He pulled Lau near the window, put a bag on his back, and held him tight. At the same moment, the clocks on Batman's bombs reached zero. The window exploded just as the police ran in. Batman pushed a button on Lau's back and a weather balloon appeared out of the bag. It flew up into the sky. Then came the sound of a very loud motor. A plane flew over and caught the balloon in its V-shaped nose. It pulled Batman and Lau from the building. Lau screamed as they were carried off into the orange sunrise.

Detective Ramirez walked into Lieutenant Gordon's office.

'Go and see what's happening outside,' she said.

Gordon ran down the stairs and out of the door. A crowd of people was on the grass, looking at a man tied up on the ground. It was Lau, and there was a sign on his chest: *Please take this man to Lieutenant Gordon.*

A few metres away, Harvey Dent was talking to newspaper reporters.

'The Chinese government is very angry about this,' said one reporter. 'What do you say to that?'

'I don't know how Mr Lau travelled here,' said Dent with a smile, 'but I'm very glad that he's back.'

Harvey Dent agreed to a plan with Lau. Lau would give him information about the Mob if Dent protected Lau and allowed him to fly back to Hong Kong. For the moment, Lau was going to stay at the police station, where Gordon could watch him.

In less than an hour, the police had caught 549 men who worked for the Mob, including Sal Maroni. This huge crowd of criminals was now in court, and Judge* Surrillo had to decide what to do with them. As she was looking through her papers, a playing card fell onto her desk. It was a joker.

Dent was in Mayor** Garcia's office across the street from the Gotham Court House.

'A lot of people will be against you now, Dent,' said the Mayor. 'Not just the Mob, but everyone who works with the Mob: politicians, reporters, police officers … Are you ready for them?'

'Yes. I'm ready,' said Dent.

BANG! A dark shape crashed into the glass in front of the Mayor's office. A dead body was hanging outside the window and it looked like Batman. His mouth was painted in a frightening clown smile.

'Oh no! Batman is dead!' cried Dent. Then he looked more carefully. The dead man, although dressed in clothes like Batman's, was thinner and shorter than Gotham's mysterious protector. He wasn't the real Batman. 'Thank God for that,' thought Dent.

The police cut the dead body down. Then Lieutenant Gordon arrived. There was a playing card on the body: a joker. Gordon read out the note on it: *Will the real Batman please say who he is? If he doesn't, more people will die.*

* Judge: a top lawyer who decides cases in a court of law

** Mayor: the head of a city's government

CHAPTER 4
'Don't you like my face?'

Detective Ramirez gave Lieutenant Gordon some papers.

'You know the joker card on the body?' she said. 'There were three fingerprints on it.'

'Any matches?' he asked.

'Yes, all three,' she said. 'They belong to Judge Surrillo, Harvey Dent and Commissioner* Loeb.'

'Oh no!' thought Gordon. 'They don't tell us who the Joker is. They tell us who he's going to kill next.'

'Send some officers to Surrillo's house,' he shouted, 'and tell Detective Wuertz to find Dent. We need to protect them. Where's Commissioner Loeb?'

'He's in City Hall.'

'Don't let anyone go in or out until I get there.'

Two police officers rang at Judge Surrillo's door.

'Gordon wants me to leave now?' she asked. 'It's very late.'

'These men are very dangerous, Judge,' said one of the officers. They led her to her car and gave her an envelope.

'This letter tells you where you're going,' they said. 'Open it before you start your car.'

The police officers drove off. Judge Surrillo didn't know that they worked for the Mob. She got into her car, opened the envelope and pulled out a piece of paper. There was only one word on it: *UP!*

A second later, her car exploded. Hundreds of playing cards flew into the air in the explosion. All of the cards were jokers.

* Commissioner: the head of the police

Lieutenant Gordon went into City Hall. There was a circle of police all around an angry Commissioner Loeb.

'What's happening here, Gordon?' he shouted.

Gordon told his men to search the building.

'I'm sorry, sir,' said Gordon as he and Commissioner Loeb walked into Loeb's office. 'We believe the Joker wants to kill you.'

'A lot of people want to kill me, Gordon,' Loeb said. 'And my answer to that problem is … drink.' He got out a glass and a bottle and poured himself a drink.

'The joker card found on the dead man had your fingerprint on it, sir,' Gordon said.

'How did they get my fingerprint?' asked Loeb. He took a long drink.

'Maybe someone took them from a glass in your house … or your office,' said Gordon. He suddenly realised. 'Wait!' he shouted.

But Loeb was already dying. He fell back, holding his throat. His drink burned the floor and made it smoke.

'Get a doctor!' shouted Gordon. But it was too late.

While Detective Wuertz was looking for Harvey Dent, Dent arrived at Bruce Wayne's party.

Soft music was playing and people were talking quietly. Suddenly a loud motor was heard above the sounds of the party. Bruce had landed on his roof. He came through the door with his arms around two beautiful women.

'Sorry I'm late,' he shouted. 'I'm so glad you started without me. But I want to say something about this party.'

He held up a large picture of Harvey Dent. 'Do you know something?' he said. 'I believe in Harvey Dent. With Dent as District Attorney, Gotham City feels safer. So please get out your cheque books. Let's make sure we keep our District Attorney around for a few more years.'

Bruce held up his glass.

'To the face of Gotham's great future – Harvey Dent.'

A little later, Bruce was standing on his rooftop when Rachel joined him. His heart jumped. He had been in love with her for years. But she had said that she could not be with him if he was Batman. It had broken his heart. Gotham needed Batman. Bruce had to be Batman until there was someone else. And that meant that he couldn't have Rachel.

'Rachel,' he said, 'Gotham City won't need Batman soon. Harvey Dent will be a wonderful new leader. A hero with a face – not like Batman.'

'You can't ask me to wait for …' Rachel began.

But Dent suddenly appeared. 'Great party, Wayne,' he said. 'Is it OK if I borrow Rachel?'

Dent led Rachel back to the party. Bruce watched them for a moment. Then he went back to the party too.

Dent took Rachel to the kitchen and shut the door.

'I feel better in here,' he said. 'Those people frighten me.'

Rachel was amazed. 'The whole Mob hates you and

you're worried about *those* people?'

'Well, being in danger is strange. It makes me see things more clearly. Now I know who I want to spend the rest of my life with. Will you marry me, Rachel?'

'I can't give you an answer, Harvey,' she replied.

Just at that moment, Bruce walked up quietly behind Dent and hit him on the head. Then he pushed him into a cupboard and put a chair against it.

'What are you doing?' Rachel asked angrily.

'The Joker's here,' said Bruce quietly. 'His men have already killed Judge Surrillo and Commissioner Loeb. Now he's looking for Harvey. Stay hidden.'

Bruce left the kitchen and went into a secret room.

The Joker was moving through the party, frightening the guests with his knife. Rachel couldn't wait in the kitchen. She had to do something. She ran towards the Joker and shouted, 'Stop!'

The Joker turned to her. 'Hello, beautiful,' he said. He held the knife to her face. 'You must be Harvey's girlfriend. You look nervous. Don't you like my face?'

He laughed like a madman and took the knife away. She hit him hard.

'Oh, you're a fighter!' said the Joker. 'I love fighters.'

'Then you'll love *me*,' said a voice.

Batman hit the Joker and grabbed the knife. But the Joker was not alone. He had come to the party with friends, and Batman had to fight them too. He had almost finished when the Joker kicked him. The pain was terrible. The Joker's shoe had another knife in it, and the knife had gone through a weak part in Batman's suit.

The Joker grabbed Rachel and pointed a gun at her head.

'Drop the gun,' said Batman.

'I will,' said the Joker, 'if you take off your mask. Show us who you are!'

Rachel shook her head at Batman.

'OK then,' said the Joker. He shot at the window, which exploded into thousands of pieces. Then he pulled Rachel over to the open space and held her out of the window – hundreds of metres above the ground.

'Let her go,' said Batman.

'Bad choice of words,' said the Joker. He opened his hand and let Rachel go.

Rachel was falling from one of Gotham's highest buildings to the ground below.

SWOOSH! Batman flew to save her but he missed. She was falling too fast.

SWOOSH! He fell faster. He caught her just as they crashed onto the roof of a taxi. They fell onto the ground. They had cuts and light injuries but they were alive.

The Joker got into his waiting car.

'What about Dent?' asked the driver.

'Dent can wait for another day,' said the Joker.

CHAPTER 5
The Joker gets closer

Alfred and Bruce were in the Bat-Bunker. Alfred could see that Bruce was extremely worried by the deaths of Judge Surrillo and Commissioner Loeb. And there was bad news about Sal Maroni too. Dent had had to let him out of prison. Was he helping the Joker now?

The Joker was clever. He wanted Batman to show his face. He wanted people to be angry with Batman. He wanted them to think that the murders were Batman's fault.

'We need to know what the Joker wants,' said Bruce.

'Perhaps this is someone that you can't understand,' said Alfred. 'Some men don't want to be rich or famous. Some men just want to make trouble. They want to watch the world burn.'

Lieutenant Gordon and Detective Ramirez ran into a flat in Orchard Street. They had heard that Harvey Dent was lying dead at this address.

Sitting at the kitchen table were two dead men. They had playing cards in their hands. All the cards were jokers. Smiles had been cut into the men's faces and their names were stuck to their chests. One man's name was Patrick Harvey. The other's was Richard Dent.

Batman arrived. Detective Ramirez shouted, 'This is your fault, Batman! They're dead because of you!'

Batman looked around the room. There it was – a bullet in the wall. He cut it out. 'I'm going to look for fingerprints on the bullet,' he said.

On the wall there was a large picture of Mayor Garcia. Someone had drawn a horrible, big red smile on him.

In the Bat-Bunker, Bruce couldn't find an exact match for the thumb print that he had found on the bullet. He asked Alfred to search while he got out his motorbike.

'Got one!' said Alfred as Bruce was getting into the lift. 'Melvin White. Criminal. 1502 Randolf Flats, near …'

Bruce didn't wait for the rest. He was soon riding his motorbike to Randolf Flats, on the other side of town.

It was the day of Commissioner Loeb's funeral and the streets were full of people. Bruce saw Rachel and Harvey sitting on a platform with Mayor Garcia and Lieutenant Gordon. There were police gunmen on every rooftop.

Mike Engel, a TV reporter, was talking in front of a camera. 'Batman has not shown us who he is,' said Engel, 'so the Joker may try to kill the Mayor today.'

Bruce rode to 1502 Randolf Flats. He ran up the stairs and kicked in the door. Inside, eight men were tied up … without their clothes. 'They took our police clothes and our guns,' one of them said.

Bruce realised that these were the men who protected the Mayor. He ran to the window but it was too late. The guards in front of the Mayor stepped forward and pointed their guns. One of them was the Joker. As they shot, Gordon jumped in front of the Mayor. People were screaming and running everywhere. The Joker and his men disappeared into the crowd.

From the platform, Harvey Dent saw that one of the Joker's men had been shot. He was now in the back of a vehicle, waiting to go to hospital. When the driver wasn't looking, Dent jumped into the front seat of the vehicle and drove away.

Barbara Gordon heard a knock at the door. Outside, there were two police officers. They told her that her husband, Lieutenant Gordon, had been killed.

She saw Batman standing not far behind the officers. 'You did this! *You*! It's all your fault!' she shouted.

Dent drove the Joker's man to an empty building and tied him to a chair. After questioning him for a few minutes, he knew who the Joker wanted to kill next. It was Rachel Dawes.

He phoned her. 'Rachel, listen to me. You're not safe. The Joker's going to kill you next. Who can you trust?'

'Bruce,' she said. 'I can trust Bruce Wayne.'

'OK,' said Dent. 'Go straight to his flat. Don't tell anyone. I'll find you there.'

After he ended the call, Dent pointed his gun at the face of the man in the chair. 'Tell me about the Joker,' he said.

The man shook his head.

'OK,' said Dent. 'Do you want to play a game?'

He took a large silver coin out of his pocket. 'Heads or tails*?' he asked. 'Heads, you live. Tails, you die.' He threw the coin into the air, caught it and pressed it into the back of his hand. Heads. 'You're lucky this time,' said Dent. 'Let's do it again.' He threw the coin again.

This time Batman caught it.

'This is wrong, Harvey,' said Batman. Don't make yourself a criminal like them.' He gave Dent back his coin.

---

* Heads is the side of a coin with a picture of a head on it. Tails is the other side. People sometimes ask 'Heads or tails?' and throw a coin. You have to guess which side will be up when the coin lands.

'Tomorrow,' he continued, 'you can tell reporters that Batman will show himself to the people of Gotham City. No one else will die because of me. Gotham is in your hands now.'

'You can't!' shouted Dent. 'You can't let them win!'

But Batman had disappeared.

Rachel and Bruce were on the rooftop of Bruce's flat.

'Harvey called me,' she said. 'He says Batman is going to tell the police who he is.'

'I have no choice,' said Bruce. 'But if I stop being Batman, we can be together, Rachel.'

'No, Bruce, we can't,' she said. 'If you go to the police, they'll send you to prison.'

Bruce knew that she was right. He went back inside.

Sadly, Rachel watched him leave. But now she knew the answer that she was going to give Harvey.

When Bruce drove off into the night, Rachel sat down to write a letter.

CHAPTER 6
Dent takes a chance

Harvey Dent was talking to a group of reporters.

'Thanks for coming, everyone,' he said. 'I'm here to tell you two things. Firstly, the police are doing everything that they can in their search for the Joker. And secondly, Batman has offered to give himself to the police.'

The crowd shouted happily. Dent saw Wayne sitting at the back of the room.

'So where is he?' asked a man.

'Well, first let's ask ourselves a question,' said Dent. 'Is it right to follow the orders of a murderer?'

'Do you think Batman's life is more important than ours?' a reporter shouted.

'Batman has sometimes broken the law,' said Dent, 'but he's also helped us to stop the criminals of this city. One day we will make Batman pay for his crimes. But not because this madman tells us to.'

The crowd realised that they weren't going to see Batman unmasked.

'No more dead cops! No more dead cops!' they shouted again and again. 'Where is Batman?'

Dent knew he had lost, but he had a plan. Wayne was beginning to stand up at the back of the room but he wasn't sure why.

'OK, OK!' shouted Dent. He offered his wrists to the police. '*I* am Batman!'

Rachel saw it all on television. She couldn't believe it. She knew that Harvey Dent wasn't Batman.

'Why is Bruce letting him do this?' she asked Alfred.

'Perhaps both Bruce and Mr Dent believe that Batman is important,' said Alfred. 'They want to save him.'

Rachel was angry. She put on her coat. She couldn't stay there while Harvey went to prison. She took an open envelope out of her bag and gave it to Alfred.

'Give this letter to Bruce when the time is right,' she said. 'Goodbye, Alfred.'

Rachel arrived at the police station as they were putting Harvey into a van. The police officers allowed them a moment together.

'This is the Joker's chance,' he said to her. 'When he attacks, Batman will kill him.'

'Please don't do this, Harvey,' she said. 'It's too dangerous.'

'I have an idea,' Dent said. He took out his lucky silver coin. 'Heads, I do this. Tails, I don't.'

'Don't leave this to chance,' said Rachel.

'I'm not,' said Harvey. He threw the coin to Rachel. She caught it and opened her hand. It was heads.

The doors closed and the van moved away. Rachel turned the coin over in her hand. It was heads. It was heads on *both* sides!

The van drove quickly through Gotham's streets. Dent was in the back with a team of special police officers. The driver had instructions not to stop for any reason. But in the middle of the street ahead was a burning truck. He slowed down and turned into a side street.

A lorry hit the van from behind. Harvey Dent smiled. The Joker's attack had begun.

SLAM! The back of another lorry crashed into the front of the van. And there was the Joker. He was shooting at the van and laughing madly. Then he took out a huge bomb thrower. He shot at the van but hit a police car instead. It exploded in a ball of fire.

Suddenly a dark form appeared. It was the Batmobile. It crashed through the fireball and flew over the other cars. But the Joker was ready to shoot again. He pointed his bomb thrower at the Batmobile.

SMASH! The back of the Batmobile exploded and the vehicle turned wildly round in circles. The Joker's laughs got louder. Finally the Batmobile stopped. For a moment nothing happened. Then the front of the Batmobile slowly changed into a motorbike – the Bat-pod. And sitting on it was Batman. The Bat-pod flew forwards as the back of the Batmobile exploded. The Bat-pod chased the lorry and the van, getting closer and closer all the time.

But the lorry went round a corner too fast. It turned over and over, then stopped moving. From under the lorry, the Joker climbed out. He was dirty but he wasn't hurt. He ran into the road and stood there in Batman's way. Batman was going too fast. He either had to hit the Joker or crash.

Batman crashed into a wall and lay on the ground. The Joker was the first to reach him. He couldn't pull off Batman's mask so he took out his knife. He was going to cut off the mask … and cut a big, red smile on his face too.

The van stopped next to them and the driver jumped out.

'Stop!' he shouted. It was Lieutenant Gordon.

Harvey Dent ran up. 'Back from the dead, Lieutenant?' he asked.

Gordon just smiled.

Lieutenant Gordon was going home to his family. His officers had taken the Joker back to the police station, and Detective Wuertz had offered to drive Harvey Dent home. It was over. Gotham was safe from the Joker's madness.

At the front door, Gordon's young son, James, ran to him.

'Did Batman save you, Dad?' he cried.

'No,' said Gordon. 'This time, I saved him.'

The phone rang and Gordon's wife, Barbara, went to answer it.

'It's for you, *Commissioner*,' she said to her husband. Gordon now had Loeb's job as head of the police. But there was a problem. Harvey Dent was missing.

Gordon drove immediately to the police station and went to see the Joker.

'Harvey Dent didn't arrive home,' he said.

'Of course not,' the Joker replied calmly.

'Where is he?' shouted Gordon.

'It depends,' said the Joker. 'He might be in one place or he might be in several places. What's the time?'

'Don't play games with me,' said Gordon. He left the room and turned off the lights.

FLICK! The lights suddenly came on again.

WHAM! The Joker's face hit the table. He looked up and saw Batman.

'Where's Dent?' asked Batman.

The Joker started to laugh.

'Where's Dent?' Batman asked again. He threw the Joker against the wall. Then he grabbed him by his neck and started to press on the Joker's throat. The Joker could only whisper.

'You'll have to play my little game if you want to save

one of them,' he said.

'Them?!' Batman went cold.

'Yes. Dent and that girlfriend of his. There are only a few minutes left. You'll have to be quick.'

'WHERE ARE THEY?' shouted Batman.

'You can only get to one of them in time,' said the Joker. 'Dent is at 250 52nd Boulevard. And Rachel is on 10th Avenue at Cicero. You'll have to choose.'

Batman hit the Joker one last time and hurried out.

The Joker was allowed by law to make one phone call. He asked for his mobile phone and pressed a button. His men were locked in another room in the police station. The stomach of one man began to shine with a blue light. He had a bomb inside him. Suddenly there was a huge explosion. No one saw the Joker as he escaped. He laughed as he disappeared into the night.

CHAPTER 7
Harvey Two Face

In a room, in the dark, Rachel Dawes was all alone. She was tied to a chair and she was frightened.

'Can anyone hear me?' she called out.

'Rachel, is that you?' It was Harvey. Where *was* he? She couldn't see him. Then she saw a speaker on the ground near her chair. Next to the speaker was a bomb. Rachel started to cry.

'It's going to be OK, Rachel,' said Harvey.

Harvey Dent was also tied to a chair. He was a long way from Rachel – in a room on the other side of town. Dent could see a bomb too. He could also see a clock counting down: 2:47 … 2:46 … . He moved his chair towards it, little by little. But suddenly his chair fell over. It knocked a can of petrol onto the floor. Harvey couldn't move. The left side of his face pressed into the wet floor and the petrol covered his face and his ear. It went into his left eye and his mouth. It felt hot.

'I want to tell you something, Harvey,' said Rachel. 'My answer is yes. I want to marry you.'

WHAM! The door crashed open. Batman was there. He'd come to rescue Rachel, but it wasn't Rachel. It was Dent! The Joker had lied. He'd given Batman the opposite addresses. Batman hoped that Commissioner Gordon reached Rachel in time.

Batman grabbed Dent and pulled him out. Behind them, there came a huge explosion. Dent's face was covered with fire, and he screamed in pain.

Commissioner Gordon was running as fast as he could to save Rachel. He was almost there. But suddenly the building exploded. He was too late! As pieces of the building fell, hundreds of playing cards flew slowly down to the ground. They were all jokers.

Rachel Dawes was dead. Batman stood at the place of her death. 'How did I let this happen?' he thought sadly.

He saw something shiny on the ground – Harvey's lucky coin. He took it to Harvey's room in Gotham General Hospital and left it on a table while he slept.

'I'm so sorry, Harvey,' he said quietly.

In Bruce Wayne's flat, Alfred read Rachel's letter again.

Dear Bruce,

I need to be honest with you. I am going to marry Harvey Dent. I love him and I want to spend the rest of my life with him. Perhaps one day Gotham won't need Batman. But I think <u>you</u> will always need Batman, Bruce.

Love now and always,

Rachel

Alfred took the letter and a cup of tea to Bruce. Bruce looked terrible.

'Rachel's death is my fault, Alfred,' he said. 'I try to make things better but I make them worse.'

'Gotham needs you,' said Alfred.

'Gotham needs a hero,' said Bruce. 'It needs Harvey Dent. And I let the Joker put him in hospital.'

Alfred took back Rachel's letter and put it in his pocket. He did not want Bruce to read it now.

Harvey Dent woke up in Gotham General Hospital. He was all alone. On the table next to his bed he saw the coin that he had given Rachel. He thought of her face, her worried smile, and felt angry. How could she be dead?

He looked again at the coin. Then he turned it over. In the explosion, the other side had turned black.

Commissioner Gordon came into the room. He could only see the right side of Dent's face. It looked fine.

'I'm sorry about Rachel,' Gordon said. Dent said nothing.

'The doctor says you're in a lot of pain, but you won't take any medicine,' Gordon went on. 'Do you …'

'What did your cops use to call me?' asked Dent.

'I don't want …' Gordon started to reply.

'SAY IT!' Dent screamed.

'Two Face,' said Gordon softly. 'Harvey Two Face.'

Dent turned his head. When Gordon saw the other side of Dent's face, he felt sick. He had never seen such terrible injuries. All the skin was burned off. His left ear was badly burned too and his eye was hanging out.

'I'm so sorry, Harvey,' he said.

'No, you're not,' Dent replied. 'Not yet.'

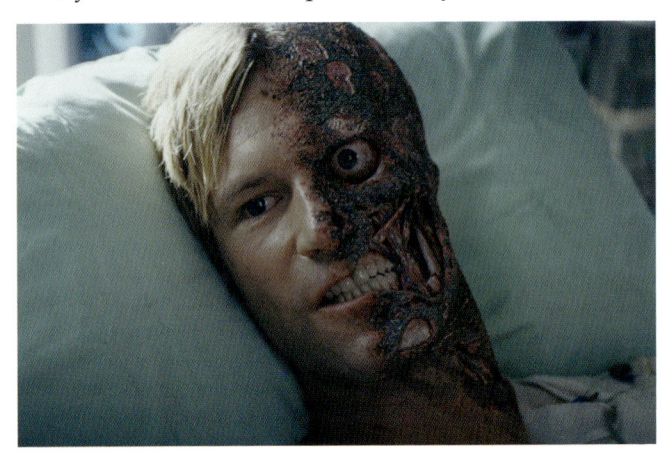

Bruce and Alfred were sitting in Bruce's flat. On a television screen behind them, people were discussing who the real Batman might be.

Suddenly a new voice cut through the conversation. 'I've put a bomb in one of the city's hospitals,' it said. Bruce and Alfred started to pay attention. 'But which hospital? You've got sixty minutes before it explodes.' Then there was a laugh … a madman's laugh. It was the Joker.

At the police station, Commissioner Gordon switched off the television.

'Call in every officer,' he shouted. 'I think the bomb's at Gotham General Hospital. Get everybody out.'

'Why Gotham General?' Detective Murphy asked.

'Because that's where Dent is,' said Gordon.

The police drove fast to Gotham General Hospital. The patients, nurses and doctors were getting onto school buses. The buses were going to drive them to safety.

A nurse came into Dent's room in the hospital.

'Hi,' she said. She pulled off her mask to show a big, blood red smile. It was the Joker.

'I wanted to see you,' the Joker said to Dent. 'I wanted to tell you that you and Rachel … it wasn't my fault. Those bombs weren't mine. I was in prison. The cops, the Mob … they are the people who did this to you.'

Dent looked at him without saying a word.

'My fight is with Gordon and Batman,' continued the Joker. 'It's not with you. They've got plans. They want law and order in Gotham. But I hate law and order.'

Dent still said nothing. The Joker turned to go.

'They're the people who put you here,' he said. 'They killed Rachel.'

The Joker walked out of the hospital and onto a waiting school bus. He pushed the button on his detonator and there was a huge explosion in the hospital. Then the bus drove off. The Joker's day of fun and games had begun.

Dent had already run out of the hospital before the explosion. He now joined Detective Wuertz in a bar.

'Hello, Detective,' he said.

Wuertz was very frightened. 'Dent!' he whispered. 'I thought you were dead.'

'Half dead,' said Dent. He turned his head to show Wuertz his ugly injuries.

'You drove *me* that night,' said Dent. 'Who drove Rachel?'

'I don't know,' said Wuertz. 'And I didn't know what they were going to do to you, I promise.'

'I don't know what I'm going to do to *you* either,' said Dent. He threw his coin. It landed black side up.

Dent pulled out his gun.

CHAPTER 8
Heads or tails, life or death?

Batman was looking at the many computer screens in front of him. Each one showed a small area of Gotham. Together, they made a complete map of the city.

'Beautiful, isn't it?' Batman said to Lucius Fox.

'Yes, but it's dangerous … and it's wrong,' said Fox. 'You've turned every phone into a microphone.'

'Not just a microphone,' said Batman. 'A camera too. Like you did in Hong Kong.'

'You're spying on thirty million people,' said Fox. 'That's not right.'

'I've got to find this man, Lucius,' said Batman. 'Please help me. You're the only person who can use this.'

Above the screens, a television came to life.

'Tonight the city will be mine,' said the Joker. 'Everybody will play by my rules. If you don't want to play, leave now.' He laughed and disappeared.

'I'll help you one last time,' Fox said to Batman.

Sal Maroni, the Mob boss, was going out for the evening. He got into the back of his huge black car.

'Who drove Rachel that night?' said a voice.

Maroni turned in surprise. Dent was sitting there in the dark … with his terrible face.

'Ask the Joker,' said Maroni.

'I'm asking you,' said Dent.

Maroni was frightened. He didn't want to die.

'It was Ramirez,' he said.

Dent got out his silver coin and threw it in the air. He caught it and looked at it. The good side was up.

'You're lucky,' he said to Maroni. 'But your driver isn't.'

Dent shot Maroni's driver, then jumped out of the car. The car went off the road and crashed into a wall.

The people of Gotham poured into the streets. They wanted to leave the city but the bridges and exit roads were closed. The police were searching them for bombs.

At the ferry station, two ferries were starting their journey away from Gotham. One carried eight hundred prisoners who had worked for the Mob. The other was full of ordinary people trying to escape the Joker's madness.

Suddenly all the lights went out on both ferries, and the radios went dead.

The first officer on the prisoner ferry went to see what the problem was. At the bottom of the ferry he found a bomb and hundreds of cans of petrol. There was a present covered in pretty paper too. He picked it up.

A mobile phone rang on the bridge of both ferries. It answered itself and they heard the voice of the Joker.

'Tonight we're going to play a little game,' he said, laughing his mad laugh. 'At midnight, I'm going to explode the bombs on both your ferries. I'll blow you out of the water. But to make things more interesting, I've given you each a little present. It's a detonator to explode the bomb on the *other* ferry. If one of you presses your button before midnight and destroys the other ferry, I'll let the people on your boat live. Decide quickly!'

Barbara Gordon answered the telephone. It was Anna Ramirez, one of her husband's detectives.

'You need to get out of the house quickly, Mrs Gordon,'

said Ramirez. 'It's not safe.'

She gave Barbara an address and said that Gordon would meet her there.

Barbara believed her.

Outside the police station, Ramirez gave the phone back to Harvey Dent. He was holding a gun to her head.

'She believed you, didn't she?' said Dent. 'Just like Rachel.'

He got out his coin and threw it into the air. It landed on the good side.

'You're lucky, officer,' he said. He hit her on the head with his gun and left. He was going to a meeting with Barbara Gordon and her children.

On the prisoner ferry, the prisoners began to shout and push. The guards pointed their guns at the crowd.

On the passenger ferry, an officer was holding the detonator. Several passengers moved towards him. They wanted to destroy the other ferry and save themselves. The officer pulled out his gun. 'Stay back!' he said.

'Let's vote,' suggested someone. '*Yes* to destroy the other ferry, and *no* to do nothing.'

Everyone was given a piece of paper.

Batman stood on a rooftop, searching the city for the Joker. 'Where is he, Fox?' he asked.

The line was silent for a moment. 'Got him,' said Fox. 'He's in the Prewitt Building.'

Batman rang Commissioner Gordon.

Batman met Gordon on the rooftop of a building opposite the Prewitt Building. Gordon's officers were already in position with their guns.

'The Joker's taken hostages,' Gordon said to Batman. 'A bus full of hospital workers and patients that went missing after Gotham General exploded.'

Batman looked into the building opposite. On the top floor, he could see the Joker's men. They were wearing clown masks and carrying guns. They were guarding a group of patients, doctors and nurses.

'We can see the five clowns clearly,' said Gordon. 'Let's shoot them.'

'Wait!' said Batman. 'It's never as simple as that with the Joker.'

'We can't wait,' said Gordon. 'If we don't move now, he'll kill everyone on the ferries.'

'Just give me five minutes,' said Batman.

'No,' said Gordon. 'There's no time.' His officers pointed their guns.

Batman jumped in front of them and flew across to the other building.

Gordon put down his gun. 'Two minutes,' he said. 'Then we shoot.'

Batman landed on the Prewitt Building. 'Fox,' he said, 'I need a picture.'

Thin pieces of special glass came down over his eyes. Now he could see into the building: the hostages, the guards … and the Joker. He was in another room, watching the ferries on the sea. In his hand was a detonator.

Batman broke the window and got inside. There was a guard around the corner. Batman hit him and the man fell to the floor. But then Batman saw something. The man's gun was taped to his hand. He pulled off his clown mask. His mouth was taped shut. It was Mike Engel, the TV reporter!

Batman looked into the next room. The other four clowns also had guns taped to their hands. But the 'patients' and 'doctors' had guns too. The difference was that their guns had bullets. *They* were the Joker's men.

'Oh no!' Batman thought. 'If the police attack, they'll shoot the wrong people.'

Batman shot his rope gun. The rope tied itself around the clowns' legs. They all fell to the floor just as the police started shooting. The police couldn't know that the clowns were good and the men dressed as hostages were bad. There was only one way to save the real hostages. Batman had to fight Gordon's officers. As the officers jumped into the building, Batman attacked them and tied them to each other. Finally he pushed them out of the window. They hung outside the building like mountain climbers who'd had an accident.

CHAPTER 9
The Dark Knight

On the passenger ferry, the pilot finished counting the votes.

'One hundred and ninety-six people said *no*,' he said. 'And three hundred and forty said *yes*.'

The passengers had voted to destroy the prisoner ferry, but they felt terrible about it. They couldn't look at each other.

The pilot of the passenger ferry looked at the detonator in his hands.

'I voted *yes*,' he said. 'But I didn't say *I*'d do it. They haven't killed us, have they?'

He put the detonator on a table and moved away. The other passengers looked at it, but no one stepped towards it.

It was ten to midnight.

On the other ferry, the prisoners were slowly moving forwards. They were pushing the guards into a corner. They had to decide quickly.

A huge prisoner walked to the front of the prison ferry.

'You don't want to die,' he said to the guard who was holding the detonator. 'But you don't want to kill anyone either. Give it to me.'

The head guard looked at the detonator, then he looked at the clock.

'The prisoners will kill you and take it anyway,' said the big prisoner. 'Give it to me. There's only one thing to do, and we need to do it now.'

In a room in the Prewitt Building, the Joker was waiting for Batman.

'How nice of you to come,' he said.

'Where's the detonator?' Batman asked.

The Joker called out. Three huge, ugly black dogs jumped onto Batman. They pushed him to the ground and bit him with their killer teeth. One by one, Batman fought them off. Then the Joker attacked him. He kicked Batman again and again with the knife in his shoe. He knew the weak places in Batman's suit, and Batman was in terrible pain.

Slowly the Joker pushed Batman towards the window, and to a deadly fall to the street below.

At one minute to midnight, a businessman on the passenger ferry walked to the front of the ferry. He picked up the detonator.

'I'll push the button,' he said. 'Those people on the other ferry are thieves and murderers. *They* should die, not us.'

He put his finger over the button. The passengers waited for the other ferry to explode, but the man couldn't do it. He put the detonator back on the table. Then he sat down with his head in his hands, ready to die.

The big prisoner took the detonator from the guard. Then he threw it out of the window, and it fell to the bottom of the sea.

It was now midnight. Batman was hanging out of the window. He couldn't hold on much longer.

'If we don't stop fighting, we're going to miss the explosions,' said the Joker. He put one foot on Batman's chest. Then he turned on the detonator, ready to destroy both ferries.

At the same moment, Batman pressed the black button on his arm.

WHOOSH! Three disks shot out, flying into the Joker's chest and arm. The Joker fell back towards the window. Batman grabbed the detonator and kicked him over the edge. But Batman had a rule. He didn't kill people. He used his rope gun and caught the Joker as he fell. Then he pulled him up like a fish on the end of a line.

'You're wrong about people,' Batman said, pointing to the ferries. 'Those people *didn't* kill each other to save themselves. There are a lot of good people out there.'

The Joker looked at Batman and smiled his crazy smile.

'Just wait until they find out about Harvey Dent,' he said. 'People won't be so good after that.'

'What did you do?' shouted Batman. He suddenly had a bad feeling about Dent.

'I took Gotham's White Knight and I destroyed him,' said the Joker. He began to laugh wildly.

Batman gave the Joker to the police. Then he called Commissioner Gordon.

Gordon didn't answer his phone. Batman knew that something must be wrong. He called Fox. 'Lucius,' he said, 'it's not over. Find Harvey Dent!'

Dent had rung Commissioner Gordon. He had asked to meet him on 52nd Street.

Gordon felt the danger as he entered the building. He took out his gun.

'Dent?' he called. There was no reply. He went up the stairs to the second floor. He was surprised to see his wife, Barbara. She was holding their two children and she was crying.

WHAM! Dent hit Gordon over the head with his gun. Gordon fell to the floor and Dent took his gun.

'Rachel died here,' Dent said. 'This is where *your* people brought her, Gordon. *Your* people.'

'I tried very hard to save her, Harvey,' said Gordon.

'But you didn't save her, did you?' said Dent. 'And now you're going to pay.'

'Please don't hurt my family!' Gordon was almost crying.

Dent pulled little James Gordon from his mother's arms.

'No! Stop!' screamed Barbara. 'Please don't!'

Dent pulled the boy to the edge of a hole in the floor.

'Please let him go,' said Gordon. 'You're right. It's my fault that Rachel died. Hurt me instead.'

'Let the boy go,' said a deep voice. Batman stepped forward.

'I'm going to give him a chance,' said Dent. 'The same chance that Rachel had.' He took out his silver coin.

'Wait!' Batman took another step towards Dent. 'It's my fault too. I chose the other address.'

Dent seemed to think about that.

'You're right,' he said. 'You go first.' He threw the coin, looked at it, and then shot Batman in the stomach. Batman fell to the floor.

'Your turn, Gordon.' Dent threw the coin again. As Dent watched the coin in the air, Batman got up and jumped on him. Dent, Batman and James disappeared through the hole in the floor. Gordon ran to the hole. Down below lay Dent. His neck was broken. Batman was holding on to a piece of wood and James was holding onto Batman. As Gordon pulled up his son, the wood broke. Batman crashed to the floor below.

Gordon ran downstairs and got on his knees beside Batman. He almost jumped out of his skin when Batman grabbed his arm.

'Thank you,' said Gordon, helping Batman to stand up. Then he looked down at Dent's broken body and his burned face. 'But the Joker has won, Batman,' he said. 'He took the best of us and destroyed him. Now the people will lose hope.'

Batman reached down. He turned Dent's head to show the good side of his face. 'People won't lose hope if they never know what Dent did,' Batman said. 'Gotham needs its hero. We can't take him away from them. The Joker cannot win.'

Gordon suddenly understood what Batman was suggesting. 'You can't say that *you* killed Wuertz and Maroni,' he said.

'Yes, I can,' said Batman. 'I have to. And it's OK, Gordon. I don't need to be a hero. I can be anything that Gotham needs me to be.'

'They'll search for you,' said Gordon.

Batman smiled. '*You*'ll search for me.'

'Why's Batman running, Dad?' asked James Gordon.
'Because we have to chase him,' his father replied. They

watched Batman jump from roof to roof as the police followed him with their dogs.

'Why, Dad? Why? He didn't do anything wrong.'

'Because Gotham needs another hero right now, James,' said Gordon. 'For the moment, Batman can only be our secret hero, our silent protector. A Dark Knight.'

THE DARK KNIGHT
THE MOVIE

Batman Begins brought Batman successfully back to the cinema in 2005. Three years later, *The Dark Knight* built on that success. It was hugely popular all over the world.

FANTASTIC ACTION SCENES

There are some great special effects in the film, but a lot of the scenes were done without them. Do you remember the scene where the huge, 18-wheel lorry turns over? That was real, and it took weeks of preparation.

IMAX cameras were used for several of the action scenes. These are difficult to use, but they show much more detail than ordinary cameras. You can see the film in an ordinary cinema or on the huge screen of an IMAX cinema.

GREAT ACTORS

Christian Bale (Batman/Bruce Wayne)

grew up in England and the US. His first acting part was in a Steven Spielberg film, *Empire of the Sun*, at the age of twelve. Bale practised fighting for two or three hours every day to prepare for the part of Batman. He even did the most difficult fighting scenes himself.

Heath Ledger (the Joker) grew up in

Australia. To prepare for his part in *The Dark Knight*, he did lots of research and thinking. Day after day he practised the Joker's voice and way of moving, and he kept a diary of the Joker's thoughts and feelings. He won several awards for the part. Sadly, *The Dark Knight* was one of his last films. He died in January 2008.

Have you ever seen an IMAX film? What was it like?

Have you seen any Batman films? What did you think of them?

Maggie Gyllenhaal (Rachel) is an

American actor from a 'movie' family. Her father is a film director and her mother a film writer. Her brother Jake is a famous actor who starred with Heath Ledger in *Brokeback Mountain*.

Michael Caine (Alfred) is a very

famous British actor. He has acted in more than 100 films and won lots of awards.

A family film!

The director of *The Dark Knight*, Christopher Nolan, wrote the screenplay with his brother Jonathan. His wife, Emma Thomas, produced the film.

What do these words mean? You can use a dictionary.

special effects   detail   scene   research   award   screenplay

BATMAN'S GADGETS OLD AND NEW!

Batman always has amazing gadgets, and in *The Dark Knight* there are some great new ones!

The new Batsuit

Batman's new suit is made from lots of pieces of tough material. Christian Bale says that it's cooler and more comfortable than the old one. The helmet isn't joined to the rest of the suit, so Batman can turn his head easily. Thin pieces of special white glass come down over Batman's eyes so he can see into buildings. There are knives hidden in the arms. And it still has its cape, which gives Batman huge bat wings to 'fly' with.

The Batmobile and the Bat-pod

The Batmobile has always been an amazing car with a lot of useful gadgets. It can climb up walls, jump across roofs and drive over anything, including traffic coming towards it! It now has GPS*, too, with a 3D map of Gotham City. And when the Batmobile is destroyed in an explosion, its front part becomes the Bat-pod. The Bat-pod is a special two-wheeled vehicle with guns and small bombs on it.

The sonar phone

Batman's mobile phone uses sound waves, just like a bat! With it, he can see through walls and into buildings ... in 3D. The phone can also send back pictures from a long way away. Towards the end of the film, Batman takes over the phones of all the people in Gotham. He makes them into cameras and microphones and they send out sound and pictures from all over the city. Batman uses them to discover where the Joker is hiding. But is it wrong to use technology to spy on people like this?

* GPS (Global Positioning System) is a gadget that tells you where you are.

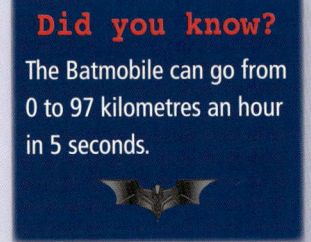

Did you know?

The Batmobile can go from 0 to 97 kilometres an hour in 5 seconds.

The Bat-pod

The new Batsuit

The Batmobile

The sonar phone

Would you like to see into buildings and hear other people's conversations like Batman? Would you like other people to see and hear *you*?!

What do these words mean? You can use a dictionary.

gadget   tough   material   helmet   cape   sonar   take over

THE DARK SIDE OF BATMAN

> 66 **Batman can only be our secret hero, our silent protector. A Dark Knight.** 99

The Dark Knight **shows a darker side to the Batman story. How did Batman become so 'dark'?**

Was Bruce a happy child?

Yes ... until he was six years old. Then a thief called Joe Chill shot his parents dead in front of him and his life changed for ever. For years he was angry and wanted revenge. Then he realised that revenge wasn't the answer. He decided to protect people and stop criminals instead. He travelled the world and learned how to fight. Then, when he was ready, he returned to Gotham City.

Why does he call himself Batman?

One day, as a child, Bruce fell down a deep well. Suddenly, hundreds of bats were flying all around him. From that moment, Bruce had a terrible fear of bats. But some years later, he taught himself not to be afraid of bats anymore. When he came back to Gotham, he used the large cave under his family home as his secret hiding place – like a bat. He became Batman.

Why are the people of Gotham City afraid of Batman?

Some people think Batman is a hero. Others think he's a dangerous vigilante because he doesn't always follow the law. With criminals, Batman uses fear instead of a gun. He knows that many people are afraid of bats. That's why he comes out at night ... when it's dark.

Why is the Joker so dangerous?

The Joker has no rules. He doesn't care about anything so he has nothing to lose. But Batman cannot become like him to fight him. He must act by his own rules, even when the Joker kills his friends and loved ones. The Joker knows this, and it gives him great power over Batman.

How did the Joker get his 'smile'?

Under the Joker's red 'smile' make-up, he has a big scar. How did he get it? The Joker tells a different story every time, but are any of his stories true?

"When I was a boy, my father thought that I was too serious. He wanted to put a smile on my face, so he cut me with a knife."

"My wife's face was scarred. She felt very sad about it. I cut my own face to make her happy again. But she didn't like my scars, so she left me."

> In what ways is Batman similar to the heroes in other action films? In what ways is he different?

What do these words mean? You can use a dictionary.

revenge   well   cave   vigilante   power   scar

PROLOGUE & CHAPTERS 1–3

Before you read

You can use your dictionary for these questions.

1 Match the words with the descriptions.

a) **bat** — i) someone who wears funny clothes and does silly things

b) **knight** — ii) someone who gives people advice about the law

c) **joker** — iii) a soldier who fought for his king and country in the past

d) **lawyer** — iv) an animal that can fly; it comes out at night

e) **clown** — v) a playing card with a funny man on it

2 Are these sentences true or false? Correct the false sentences.

a) A **mask** is something that you wear on your feet.

b) You can press a **button** to start or stop a machine.

c) A **balloon** is filled with air.

d) **Bombs** are often used in children's games.

3 Complete the sentences with these words.

explode   grab   mark   security   signal   system   trust

a) He stopped to ... his hat and coat, then ran out of the house.

b) It takes a long time to go through airport ... these days. They even search your shoes!

c) On our menu, we ... all the vegetarian dishes with a V.

d) I've know him for a long time and I ... him completely.

e) Let's go! That bomb might ... at any minute!

f) It's like a freezer in here! The central heating ... isn't working.

g) Before turning left, cyclists should make a ... to other traffic with their left arm.

After you read

4 Why are these people important to Bruce Wayne?

Rachel   Alfred   Lucius

5 Answer the questions.
  a) What do you know about the Joker?
  b) How do the marked bank notes help the police?
  c) What is different about Batman's new Batsuit?
  d) Why do Bruce and Lucius go to Hong Kong?

6 What do you think?
  a) Which people in the story don't you trust?
  b) Who do you think Rachel will choose in the end, Bruce Wayne or Harvey Dent?

CHAPTERS 4–6

Before you read
7 Match the two halves of the sentences.
  a) A **bullet**   **i)** happens after someone dies.
  b) A **hero**   **ii)** is used to pay for things.
  c) A **coin**   **iii)** fights the bad guys.
  d) A **fingerprint** **iv)** comes out of a gun.
  e) A **funeral**   **v)** is often left on something after you have touched it.

8 Guess the answers. Then read and check.
  a) Will Batman say who he is?
  b) What will happen if he doesn't?
  c) Who will the Joker try to kill next?

After you read
9 Are these sentences true or false? Correct the false sentences.
  a) Bruce has a party to celebrate his birthday.
  b) At the funeral, the Joker pretends to be a police guard.
  c) If Bruce stops being Batman, he can be with Rachel.
  d) When the Batmobile is destroyed, Batman has to walk.
  e) At the police station, Batman questions the Joker in a friendly way.

10 What do you think?

    a) What kinds of people are at Bruce's party? Would you like to be at a party with people like that?

    b) Who will Batman try to save, Rachel or Harvey Dent?

CHAPTERS 7–9

Before you read

11 Are these sentences true or false? Correct the false sentences.

    a) A **ferry** is a ship that takes people from one place to another.

    b) You can use a **rope** to tie things or for climbing.

    c) You use a **detonator** to make a bomb safe.

    d) A **hostage** is a person who guards prisoners.

After you read

12 Complete the sentences with the correct name.

    a) … rescues Harvey Dent before the explosion.

    b) … tries to save Rachel but is too late.

    c) … reads Rachel's letter to Bruce.

    d) …, … and … go to see Harvey Dent in hospital.

13 Number these sentences in the correct order.

    a) The people on one ferry vote to destroy the other ferry.

    b) The two ferries start their journey from Gotham.

    c) A prisoner throws a detonator out of the window.

    d) Batman stops the Joker from destroying the ferries.

    e) A businessman tries to push the button, but can't.

    f) The Joker phones the ferries to explain his new 'game'.

14 Why is Harvey angry with these people? Who does he kill?

    Wuertz   Maroni   Ramirez   Gordon   Batman

15 What do you think?

    a) Do you like the way the story ends? If you do, say why. If you don't, say how you would like it to end.

    b) Why is the book (and the last chapter) called *The Dark Knight*? Can you think of a different title?